DINOSAURS
OF THE UPPER CRETACEOUS

DAVID & OLIVER WEST

FIREFLY BOOKS

A FIREFLY BOOK

Published by Firefly Books Ltd. 2016

First printing

Publisher Cataloging-in-Publication Data (U.S.)

Names: West, David, 1956-, author.
Title: Dinosaurs of the Upper Cretaceous : 25 dinosaurs / David West.
Description: Richmond Hill, Ontario, Canada : Firefly Books, 2016. | Series: Dinosaurs. | Includes
   index. | Summary: "An illustrated guide of 25 of the best-known dinosaurs of the period,
   providing up-to-date information with highly detailed computer generated artwork. Illustrated
   introductory spreads provide background information on the time periods in which the
   dinosaurs lived" -- Provided by publisher.
Identifiers: ISBN 978-1-77085-837-4 (paperback) | 978-1-77085-838-1 (hardcover)
Subjects: LCSH: Dinosaurs – Juvenile literature.
Classification: LCC QE861.5W478 |DDC 567.9 – dc23

Library and Archives Canada Cataloguing in Publication

West, David, 1956-, author
        Dinosaurs of the upper Cretaceous : 25 dinos... / David West.
(Dinosaurs)
Includes index.
ISBN 978-1-77085-838-1 (hardback).--ISBN 978-1-77085-837-4 (paperback)
        1. Dinosaurs--Juvenile literature. 2. Paleontology--Cretaceous--
Juvenile literature. I. Title.
QE861.5.W4693 2016   j567.9   C2016-902144-0

Published in the United States by
Firefly Books (U.S.) Inc.
P.O. Box 1338, Ellicott Station
Buffalo, New York 14205

Published in Canada by
Firefly Books Ltd.
50 Staples Avenue, Unit 1
Richmond Hill, Ontario L4B 0A7

Printed in China

Text by David and Oliver West
Illustrations by David West

Produced by David West
Children's Books,
6 Princeton Court, 55 Felsham
Road, London SW15 1AZ

CONTENTS

The Upper Cretaceous 4

ALBERTOSAURUS 6

ALIORAMUS 7

ANKYLOSAURUS 8

ANTARCTOSAURUS 9

AUSTRORAPTOR 10

CARNOTAURUS 11

CITIPATI 12

CORYTHOSAURUS 13

DASPLETOSAURUS 14

DEINOCHEIRUS 15

EDMONTOSAURUS 16

GIGANTORAPTOR 17

LAMBEOSAURUS 18

19 MAIASAURA

20 MONONYKUS

21 PACHYCEPHALOSAURUS

22 PARASAUROLOPHUS

23 PENTACERATOPS

24 PROTOCERATOPS

25 TARBOSAURUS

26 THERIZINOSAURUS

27 TRICERATOPS

28 TROODON

29 TYRANNOSAURUS

30 VELOCIRAPTOR

31 Glossary

32 Index

THE UPPER CRETACEOUS

The Upper Cretaceous lasted from 89 to 65 million years ago. It was a warm period with no ice caps at the poles. Sea levels reached their highest ever during this time. This meant that most of the midwest United States and parts of Europe were under water. The Atlantic Ocean widened as North and South America drew away from Africa and Europe.

The first of many leafy trees, including figs and magnolias, appeared. Flowering plants spread, helped by the arrival of bees. Dinosaurs were at their most diverse stage with most types living during this period. This was also the time when *Tyrannosaurus rex* walked the Earth.

The Cretaceous period ended with the most famous mass extinction in history, which killed all the dinosaurs. Many other animal groups were also lost, including pterosaurs, ammonites, mosasaurs and plesiosaurs. Scientists think the cause was a large asteroid that slammed into the Earth along with intense volcanic activity during the end of this period.

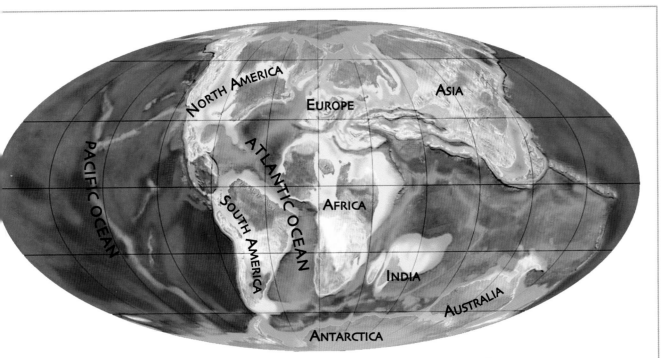

This map shows the Earth at the time of the Cretaceous period, 90 million years ago. Below, a scene from the North American Cretaceous, 70 million years ago, shows a pair of Edmontosauruses (1) and a Euoplocephalus (2) feeding on flowering plants at the edge of a river. A family of Pachyrhinosauruses (3) flee from a hungry Albertosaurus (4).

ALBERTOSAURUS

Albertosaurus, named after where it was found in Alberta, Canada, was a bipedal predator with strong muscular legs and small two-fingered arms. It was a meat-eating **theropod** and a relative of *Tyrannosaurus*. It had two small horns above its eyes that may have been only for display purposes. The discovery of multiple fossils at a single site suggests these dinosaurs may have lived in packs.

Albertosaurus lived around **70 million years ago**. Fossil remains have been found in Canada, North America. It grew up to 30 feet (9.1 m) long and weighed approximately 2.2 tons (2 tonnes).

ALIORAMUS

Alioramus, meaning "different branch," was a **tyrannosaur**, belonging to the same family as *Albertosaurus* and *Tyrannosaurus*. *Alioramus* is characterized by its five bony protrusions on the top of its snout. It also had more teeth (76 to 78) than any other **tyrannosaur**. Tyrannosaurus had approximately 60.

Alioramus lived around **70 million years ago**. Fossil remains have been found in the Gobi Desert in Mongolia, Asia. It grew up to 20 feet (6 m) long.

ANKYLOSAURUS

Ankylosaurus means "fused lizard." It gets its name from the bony nodules embedded (fused) into its leathery hide. It gives its name to the family of armored dinosaurs called **ankylosaurs**. *Ankylosaurus* was so well armored that it even had armor-plated eyelids. It also had a large bony club on the end of its tail. It used this as a weapon against predators such as *Tyrannosaurus* (see page 29). Its only weak point was its underside. If a predator managed to flip *Ankylosaurus* on its back it was defenseless.

Ankylosaurus lived **74–67 million years ago**. Fossil remains have been found in Canada and the United States, North America. It grew up to 23 feet (7 m) long and weighed around 5.8 tons (5.3 tonnes).

Despite its name, the *Antarctosaurus* was not found in Antarctica. It was found in Argentina, South America, and the name means "southern lizard." *Antarctosaurus* was an extremely large **sauropod**, known as a **titanosaur**. A complete skeleton of *Antarctosaurus* has never been discovered. Two upper thigh bones have been found that are 7.7 feet (2.35 m) in length. This suggests that the *Antarctosaurus* could have been as heavy as 80 tons (72.5 tonnes).

Antarctosaurus lived around **83–80 million years ago**. Fossil remains have been found in Argentina, South America. It is estimated to have been 37 to 80 tons (33.5–72.5 tonnes) in weight but its length is unknown.

AUSTRORAPTOR

Austroraptor, meaning "southern thief," was one of the largest **dromaeosaurs** found in the Southern Hemisphere. They had short forearms, conical-shaped teeth and weak biting muscles, which suggests they hunted smaller prey. They may also have fed on aquatic prey, using their sickle toe to strike out at fish in shallow water, and grabbing the slippery meal with their teeth.

Austroraptor lived approximately **70 million years ago**. Fossil remains have been found in Argentina, South America. It grew up to 17 feet (5.2 m) long and weighed up to 500 pounds (227 kg).

CARNOTAURUS

Carnotaurus was a large, lightly built **theropod** of the **abelisaur** family. Its name means "meat(-eating) bull," because of its carnivorous nature and the horns above its eyes. It may have used its horns to fight other *Carnotauruses* in mating rituals. Its tiny arms were of no practical use. It would have attacked and killed its prey with its jaws, which were crammed full of sharp teeth.

Carnotaurus lived **72–69 million years ago**. Fossil remains have been found in Argentina, South America. It grew up to 29.5 feet (9 m) long and weighed around 1.1 tons (1 tonne).

CITIPATI

Citipati was one of the largest members of the **oviraptor** family of **theropod** dinosaurs. It had a long neck and a short tail. It was covered in feathers. It had a bony crest on its head similar to modern day cassowary birds. Its name means "funeral pyre lord," after a Buddhist god.

Citipati lived **81–75 million years ago**. Fossil remains have been found in Mongolia, Asia. It grew up to 10 feet (3 m) long and weighed around 500 pounds (227 kg).

CORYTHOSAURUS

The "helmet lizard" was a large, plant-eating dinosaur of the **hadrosaur** family, referred to as duck-billed dinosaurs. The large crest on *Corythosaurus*' head gives it its name. The crest had hollow chambers and it is likely that it was used to make low-pitched sounds, similar to a trombone, to communicate with other members of its herd. Although these dinosaurs could stand up on their two hind legs they usually walked on all fours.

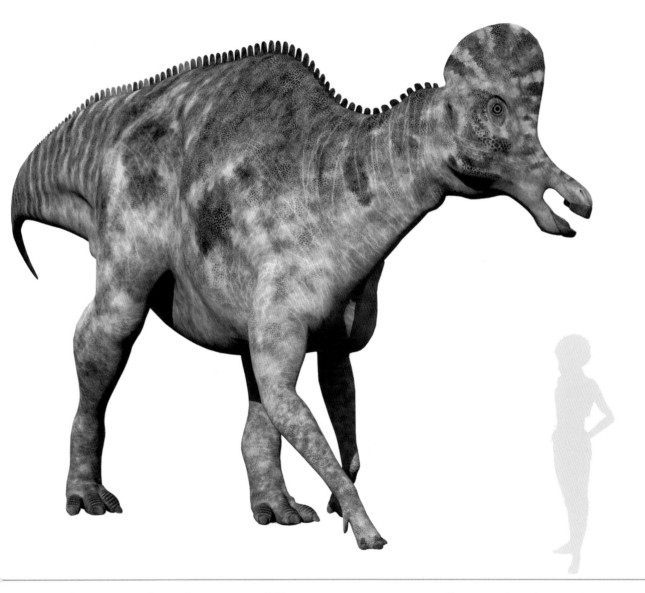

Corythosaurus lived **77–75 million years ago**. Fossil remains have been found in Canada, North America. It grew up to 29.5 feet (9 m) long and weighed around 4.2 tons (3.8 tonnes).

DASPLETOSAURUS

Daspletosaurus, meaning "frightful lizard," was a meat-eating **theropod** of the **tyrannosaur** family. It would have preyed upon **hadrosaurs** such as *Brachylophosaurus*, the **ceratopsians** *Coronosaurus* and *Albertaceratops*, as well as **pachycephalosaurs**, **ornithomimosaurs** and possibly **ankylosaurs**.

Daspletosaurus lived around **77–74 million years ago**. Fossil remains have been found in Canada, North America. It grew up to 29.5 feet (9 m) long and weighed around 2.7 tons (2.5 tonnes).

DEINOCHEIRUS

Deinocheirus was an unusual **ornithomimosaur**, with the largest arms of any bipedal dinosaur at 7.9 feet (2.4 m) long. Its name means "horrible hand" because of the large, blunt claws on its three-fingered hands. It had relatively short legs, and its vertebrae had tall spines that formed a sail along its back. It had a long, narrow skull and was probably an omnivore that fed on plants and fish. Its claws may have been used for digging and for gathering plants.

Deinocheirus lived around **70 million years ago**. Fossil remains have been found in Mongolia, Asia. It grew up to 36 feet (11 m) long and weighed around 6.5 tons (5.9 tonnes).

EDMONTOSAURUS

Edmontosaurus, meaning "Edmonton lizard," was a duck-billed dinosaur known as a **hadrosaur**. They were slow-moving herbivores that ate conifers and other vegetation, and had very few defenses against predators. Unlike most dinosaurs, the *Edmontosaurus* could chew, grinding vegetation to a pulp before swallowing. This would have helped it to digest its food.

Edmontosaurus lived between **73–66 million years ago**. Fossil remains have been found in Canada and the United States, North America. It could grow up to 39 feet (11.9 m) long and weighed 4.4 tons (4 tonnes).

GIGANTORAPTOR

Gigantoraptor, meaning "giant thief," was a member of the **oviraptors**. It was 35 times more massive than the heaviest oviraptor previously discovered, *Citipati* (see page 12). This huge, bird-like dinosaur had a horny beak and was probably an omnivore. It had long hind legs and large claws and would have been fast enough to outrun any predators.

Gigantoraptor lived **90–85 million years ago**. Fossil remains have been found in Mongolia, Asia. It grew up to 26 feet (7.9 m) long and weighed around 1.5 tons (1.4 tonnes).

LAMBEOSAURUS

Meaning "Lambe's lizard," *Lambeosaurus* was named after the paleontologist, Lawrence Lambe. It was a **hadrosaur** dinosaur, similar to *Corythosaurus* (see page 13) although its crest, resembling a hatchet, was quite different. Although the purpose of the crest is unknown, scientists think it may have been used to amplify sounds or as a visual signaling device to other members of the herd, or possibly both.

Lambeosaurus lived **76–75 million years ago**. Fossil remains have been found in Canada, the United States and Mexico, North America. It grew up to 29.5 feet (9 m) long and weighed around 4.2 tons (3.8 tonnes).

MAIASAURA

Maiasaura, meaning "caring mother lizard," was a large, plant-eating, duck-billed dinosaur. These gentle **hadrosaurs** lived in vast herds that may have numbered 10,000 individuals. Fossil remains of nesting sites show that *Maiasauras* looked after their young after they had hatched. Nests were packed closely together in colonies, like those of modern seabirds. The space between the nests was only 23 feet (7 m) which was significantly less than the length of the adult animal. The nests were made of earth and contained around 30 to 40 eggs.

Maiasaura lived around **80–75 million years ago**. Fossil remains have been found in the United States, North America. It grew up to 29.5 feet (9 m) long and weighed around 5.5 tons (5 tonnes).

MONONYKUS

This strange little **theropod** dinosaur had a pair of short arms, each of which had only one finger and a 3 inch (7.6 cm) long claw. Its name means "one claw." Scientists think *Mononykus* may have used its claws to dig into termite nests to pull out the insects to eat. Its large eyes suggest that it might have fed at night when there were fewer predators about.

Mononykus lived around **70 million years ago**. Fossil remains have been found in Mongolia, Asia. It grew up to 3.3 feet (1 m) long and weighed around 19.8 pounds (9 kg).

PACHYCEPHALOSAURUS

Pachycephalosaurus, meaning "thick-headed lizard," was a bird-hipped dinosaur famous for having a bony, domed skull, up to 10 inches (25.4 cm) thick. Its head and snout were covered in short spikes and it had a small beak for cropping plants. It had good vision and could run quickly to escape predators. Male *Pachycephalosauruses* would flank-butt their rivals in mating contests.

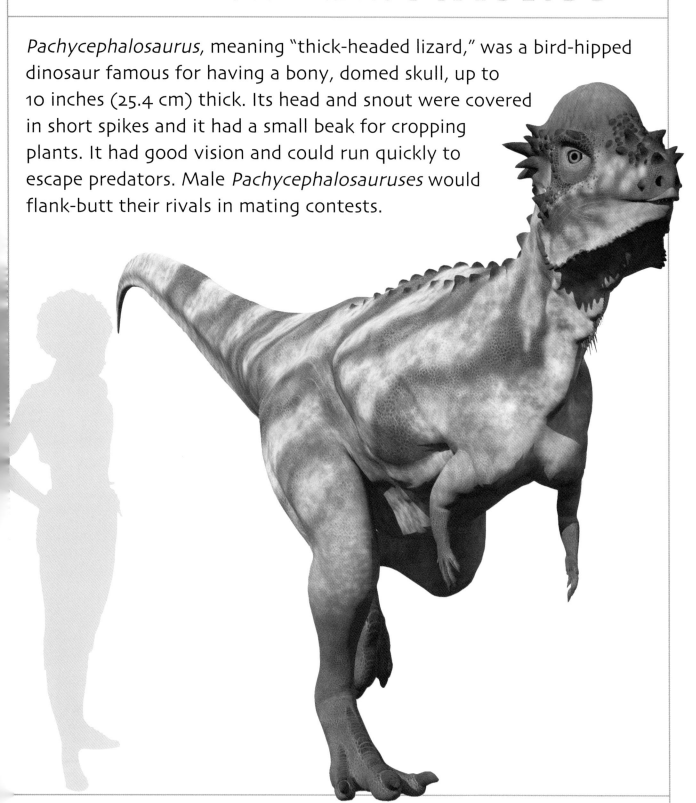

Pachycephalosaurus lived **70–66 million years ago**. Fossil remains have been found in the United States, North America. It grew up to 9.8 feet (3 m) long and weighed around 254 pounds (115.2 kg).

PARASAUROLOPHUS

Parasaurolophus was a plant-eating dinosaur of the **hadrosaur** family. Its name means "near crested lizard." It had a large, hollow, bony crest growing out in a curve from the back of its skull. Like other crested **hadrosaurs** such as *Corythosaurus* (see page 13), the crest was probably used for amplifying sound and communication. Like other **hadrosaurs** it could walk on either two legs or four. It probably preferred to walk and feed on four legs, but to run from predators on two.

Parasaurolophus lived **76–73 million years ago**. Fossil remains have been found in Canada and the United States, North America. It grew up to 31.2 feet (9.5 m) long and weighed around 2.8 tons (2.5 tonnes).

PENTACERATOPS

Pentaceratops was a large, horned dinosaur of the **ceratopsian** family. Its name means "five-horned face," after its five horns — one nose horn, two eye horns and two cheek horns. It had a very tall frill that was adorned with sharp, pointed spikes. This made a fearsome sight to put off predators and may also have acted as a display during courtship.

Pentaceratops lived **76–73 million years ago**. Fossil remains have been found in the United States, North America. It grew up to 22.3 feet (6.8 m) long and weighed around 4.4 tons (4 tonnes).

Protoceratops, an early **ceratopsian**, is affectionately known as the "sheep of the Gobi." Large numbers of their fossils have been found in the Gobi Desert of Mongolia in Asia, suggesting that they lived in herds. Their large neck frill is thought to have been used as a display to impress potential mates. They were herbivores, and their beaks were used to slice through the tough tubers and roots they dug up. They had long legs that would enable them to run quickly to escape predators.

Protoceratops lived around **75–71 million years ago**. Fossil remains have been found in the Gobi Desert of Mongolia in Asia. It grew up to 6 feet (1.8 m) long and could weigh up to 400 pounds (181.4 kg).

TARBOSAURUS

Tarbosaurus, meaning "alarming lizard," was a meat-eating **theropod** of the **tyrannosaur** family. Like *Tyrannosaurus* (see page 29) it had small forelimbs with only two fingers on each. *Tarbosaurus'* eyes did not face directly forward like *Tyrannosaurus'* did, which suggests that it lacked the binocular vision of a true hunter. *Tarbosaurus* probably fed on large **hadrosaurs** such as *Saurolophus* and *Barsboldia*, **sauropods** such as *Nemegtosaurus* and *Opisthocoelicaudia*, and the large **ornithomimosaur**, *Deinocheirus* (see page 15).

Tarbosaurus lived around **70 million years ago**. Fossil remains have been found in Mongolia and China, Asia. It grew up to 39 feet (11.9 m) long and weighed around 5.5 tons (5 tonnes).

THERIZINOSAURUS

Therizinosaurus was a strange-looking **theropod** dinosaur with enormous hands that ended in claws shaped like scythes. Its name means "reaping lizard," after these claws. It may have been an omnivore, feeding on the leaves of plants and supplementing its diet with termites, using its giant claws to rake open the termite mounds. Its claws would have been an effective defense against almost any predator foolish enough to take it on.

Therizinosaurus lived around **70 million years ago**. Fossil remains have been found in Mongolia, Asia. It grew up to 33 feet (10 m) long and weighed around 3.3 tons (3 tonnes).

TRICERATOPS

Triceratops, meaning "three-horned face," was a herbivorous **ceratopsian** dinosaur. Its frill at the back of its head and its horns were probably used for courtship displays. Its horns were also used for defense, since there is fossil evidence of partially healed *Tyrannosaurus* tooth marks on a *Triceratops*' brow horn. Its numerous teeth suggest it ate large amounts of fibrous plants such as ferns, palms and cycads.

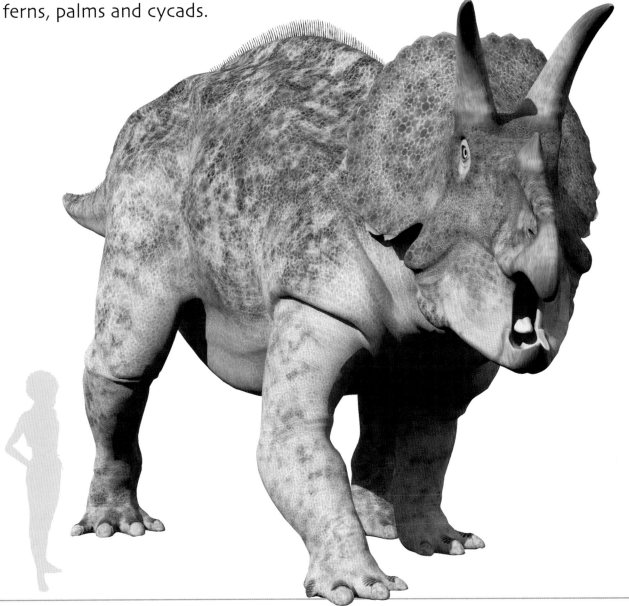

Triceratops lived **67–65 million years ago**. Fossil remains have been found in the United States, North America. It grew up to 29.5 feet (9 m) long and weighed around 6.6 tons (6 tonnes).

TROODON

Troodon was a relatively small, bird-like, **theropod** dinosaur. Its name means "wounding tooth," after its unusual teeth. It was probably an omnivore, feeding on plants and hunting small mammals and lizards. It had forward-facing eyes, grasping hands and large, retractable, sickle-shaped claws on its second toes, which were raised off the ground when it ran.

Troodon lived around **77 million years ago**. Fossil remains have been found in Canada and the United States, North America. It grew up to 6.6 feet (2 m) long and weighed around 110 pounds (50 kg).

TYRANNOSAURUS

The "tyrant lizard" was a strongly built **theropod** and the largest of the **tyrannosaurs**. Its jaw was crammed with teeth, 6 inches (15.2 cm) long, with serrated edges. It could crush bones and tear off chunks of meat — and swallow it all whole.

Tyrannosaurus lived **67–65 million years ago**. Fossil remains have been found in Canada and the United States, North America. It grew up to 39 feet (11.9 m) long and weighed around 7.5 tons (6.8 tonnes).

VELOCIRAPTOR

Velociraptor was a small member of the **dromaeosaur** family of bird-like **theropod** dinosaurs. It was a bipedal, feathered carnivore with a long tail and, like all **dromaeosaurs**, it had a large, sickle-shaped claw on each foot. It was fast, ferocious and hunted in packs. Its name means "swift seizer." One famous fossil shows a *Velociraptor* locked in combat with a *Protoceratops*.

Velociraptor lived around **75–71 million years ago**. Fossil remains have been found in Mongolia, Asia. It grew to an estimated 6 feet (1.8 m) long and weighed around 33 pounds (15 kg).

GLOSSARY

abelisaur
A family of ceratosaur-like theropod dinosaurs that included *Abelisaurus*, *Carnotaurus* and *Majungasaurus*, which thrived during the Cretaceous period.

ankylosaur
A family of bulky, quadrupedal, armored dinosaurs that had a club-like tail. The family included *Ankylosaurus* and *Euoplocephalus*.

ceratopsian
A member of a group of herbivorous, beaked dinosaurs with frilled collars. Members included *Pentaceratops* and *Triceratops*.

dromaeosaur
A family of bird-like theropod dinosaurs, with a large, curved claw on the second toe, which included the famous *Velociraptor*.

hadrosaur
A family of duck-billed dinosaurs that included *Edmontosaurus* and *Parasaurolophus*.

ornithomimosaur
A family of theropod dinosaurs that looked like modern ostriches, which included *Pelecanimimus*, *Gallimimus* and *Deinocheirus*.

oviraptor
A family of bird-like, omnivorous dinosaurs with toothless, parrot-like beaks and bony crests. The family included *Citipati* and *Gigantoraptor*.

pachycephalosaur
A family of bipedal, herbivorous dinosaurs with thick, domed skulls. Members included *Stegoceras* and *Pachycephalosaurus*.

sauropod
A group of large, four-legged, herbivorous dinosaurs with long necks and long tails. This group included the well-known *Brachiosaurus*, *Diplodocus* and *Apatosaurus*.

theropod
The large group of lizard-hipped dinosaurs that walked on two legs and included most of the giant carnivores such as *Tyrannosaurus*.

titanosaur
A family of sauropod dinosaurs that included some of the heaviest animals ever to walk the Earth such as *Argentinosaurus*.

tyrannosaur
A family of carnivorous theropod dinosaurs that included the famous *Tyrannosaurus rex*.

INDEX

Africa 4, 5
Albertaceratops 14
Albertosaurus 5, 6, 7
Alioramus 7
ankylosaurs 8, 14
Ankylosaurus 8
Antarctica 5, 9
Antarctosaurus 9
Argentina 9, 10, 11
Austroraptor 10

Brachylophosaurus 14

Canada 6, 8, 13, 14, 16, 18, 22, 28, 29
Carnotaurus 11
ceratopsian 14, 23, 24, 27
Citipati 12, 17
communication 22
Coronosaurus 14
Corythosaurus 13, 18, 22

Daspletosaurus 14
Deinocheirus 15, 25
dromaeosaur 30

Edmontosaurus 5, 16
Euoplocephalus 5
Europe 4, 5

Gigantoraptor 17

hadrosaur 13, 14, 16, 18, 19, 22, 25

Lambeosaurus 18

Maiasaura 19
Mongolia 7, 12, 15, 17, 20, 24, 25, 26, 30
Mononykus 20

omnivore 15, 17, 26, 28
ornithomimosaur 14, 15
oviraptor 12, 17

pachycephalosaur 14
Pachycephalosaurus 21
Pachyrhinosaurus 5
Parasaurolophus 22
Pentaceratops 23
plants 4, 5, 15, 21, 26, 28
Protoceratops 24

sauropod 9
South America 4, 5

Tarbosaurus 25
Therizinosaurus 26

theropod 6, 11, 12, 14, 20, 25, 26, 28, 29, 30
titanosaur 9
Triceratops 27
Troodon 28
tyrannosaur 7, 14, 25, 29
Tyrannosaurus 4, 6, 7, 8, 25, 27, 29

United States 4, 8, 16, 18, 19, 21, 22, 23, 27, 28, 29

Velociraptor 30